Chichester

in old picture postcards

by
Kenneth Green

European Library – Zaltbommel/Netherlands

About the author:
Ken Green was born and educated in Chichester where he works as a building consultant. His interest in the city's past extends back to the war years when he was a pupil at Chichester Boys' High School.

Together with his wife Sheila, also a Cicestrian, he was one of the founders of Chichester Local History Society and he has been its honorary secretary since 1982. He has broadcast on local radio and given talks to many societies throughout West Sussex.

This is Ken's third book about his home town and it is drawn from his own personal collection of postcards and pictures as well as from those of other members of the Society.

GB ISBN 90 288 5383 9 / CIP

© 1992 European Library – Zaltbommel/Netherlands

No part of this book may be reproduced in any form, by print, photoprint, microfilm or any other means, without written permission from the publisher.

INTRODUCTION

In recent years there have been several books published containing pictures from Chichester's past. They have all been enthusiastically received, both by the older inhabitants, who can remember many of the features illustrated, and by more recent residents, who wish to learn about the city as it once was.

European Library have published similar books for many towns throughout Europe, over 500 of them in the United Kingdom. It is unthinkable that such an historic city as Chichester should not be included in their series and so I was delighted when they invited me to produce this present volume.

The collecting of picture postcards is reputed to be the second most popular hobby in both Europe and America, stamp collecting being the first. The earliest cards date from the late Victorian era and cover nearly every conceivable subject.

The picture postcard occupied a special place in peoples' lives at the turn of the century, before the days of the telephone. For a halfpenny one could send a message that would be delivered the next day. Cards could be used to send a brief item of news, a birthday greeting or to confirm the details of a forthcoming visit.

As today, cards were sent by those on holiday and it is clear by reading some of the cards that Chichester was a busy tourist centre, the Cathedral and the Market Cross being the most popular subjects.

Institutions such as the Bishop Otter Teacher Training College often provided cards for the students to write home on and almost every aspect and room of the college can be found on these cards. On one, dated June 1910, I discovered that the girls were given an afternoon off, apparently as 10,000 troops were engaged in maneuvres on the Downs to the north of Chichester. Others tell of home-sickness and exams. Sometimes the message is more interesting as a comment on life at the time, than the picture itself.

Local photographers such as Walter Malby, whose studio was in East Street; Arthur Morey of St. Pancras and Thomas Russell of Southgate, all produced postcards illustrating local events and personalities. They seemed happy to print cards that could only have had a very small circulation. These are now the most sought after items for the enthusiast, studying local history.

W.H. Barratt's, the stationers, whose shop by the Cross can be seen in many of the cards, competed with the more famous national publishers of postcards, such as: Raphael Tuck, Valentines and Frith, in providing pictures of the city's landmarks for the visitor.

Also rare, but of great local interest, are the advertising cards given out by shopkeepers and other tradesmen to promote their business.

In addition to the teacher training college mentioned earlier, there were other institutions that became the subject of postcards. Soldiers at the Barracks and patients at the Royal West Sussex and Graylingwell Hospitals sent cards depicting their establishments. Many of these cards have survived to be returned to their town of origin. Graylingwell was used as a military hospital during the First World War and the cards sent home by patients were often the first news to be received in many months by anxious relatives.

As far as is possible I have tried to include in the succeeding pages only pictures that have not previously been published in other books. I would like to acknowledge the debt I owe to those who have lent me, or let me copy, their pictures, particularly to Alfred Sivyer who had the foresight to start his collection before postcard-collecting became so popular (and expensive!) and who generously let me take my pick from it. Finally to my wife, Sheila, for anyone who has undertaken a similar project, will appreciate the help and tolerance required from one's partner during its production.

1. The building that most visitors remember and associate with Chichester is the Market Cross. It was built in 1501 and given to the citizens of Chichester by Bishop Edward Storey to provide them with a place under cover to sell their wares. This picture, taken from South Street at the turn of the century, shows Charge's drapery shop, in the distance the sign of the Anchor Inn in North Street can be seen.

2. The four main streets of Chichester radiate from the Cross, the series of pictures that follow, depict these streets over the last century. In this 1936 picture of North Street one can see Bull's hardware shop on the left and Turner's shoe shop is in the building formerly occupied by The Anchor. In these pictures, it is always surprising to note the amount of advertising that was written on the walls of buildings. Thankfully this is a feature that has mostly disappeared.

3. This earlier picture was taken a little further along North Street in about 1890. Certainly it was before the advent of the motor car. There is an interesting truck by the pavement on the left, possibly for carrying sacks or, as it is outside the premises of Lambert & Norris the brewers, maybe barrels. Egbert Moore at No. 21, is described in the directories of the time as an outfitter and house furnisher. It is also noted that he owned a pawnbroker's shop in Chapel Street.

4. A 1930's postcard taken in East Street. A street trader is seen to be selling vegetables outside what was then the Westminster Bank. T.E. Jay's, the ironmongers, are still remembered by many of the city's older residents. The shop has now made way for the Tesco Supermarket, although the family name is still to be seen in the Jay Walk shopping arcade in St. Martin's Street.

5. East Street in 1912. One of the early effects of the motor car upon city life can be seen on the left, where A.T. Humphry has opened his garage in what by today's standards would be seen as a most unsuitable site. Rogers and Sons' premises were a popular restaurant. They also ran a hotel on the upper floors of the building. Another well-known Chichester business can be seen on the extreme right, Storry's musical shop, later to be re-located to North Street.

6. This view of South Street was taken one hundred years ago. It is remarkable how little it has changed in that time, for certainly, all of the buildings on the left can be seen today. The horse-drawn carriages have plates indicating that they were probably hired vehicles making their way to and from the railway station.

7. A little further down South Street and fifty years later than in the last picture. The Congregational Church, that can be seen on the left, was completed in 1893. It is one of the many places of worship within the city that have been demolished in recent years. The building to the right of it was at one time Chitty's mineral water factory and depot, but by the time of this postcard, it was occupied by Field's Garages. Unusually, there is no sign of any traffic in the picture although some evidence of horses will be spotted by the sharp-eyed reader.

8. To complete our tour of the main streets, this turn-of-the-century view of West Street shows the railings which surrounded the Cathedral churchyard until they were removed in 1941 to help in the war effort. We can also see two good examples of the city's gas lights. The citizens of Chichester had always been proud of the fact that they achieved street lighting in 1823, a week before it appeared in Portsmouth.

9. As long ago as Roman times, Chichester's East Gate was the major entrance to the city. It was therefore appropriate that Eastgate Square should be chosen, after the First World War, to site the City's memorial to the fallen. In this picture General Robertson has just unveiled the memorial in the presence of the City Council and a crowd that would have included many ex-servicemen. The memorial was later inscribed with the names of the fallen in the Second World War and in the 1950's was moved to its present site in the Litten Gardens off St. Pancras.

10. Among the businesses in Eastgate Square, was Alfred Triggs' Furnishing Store, demolished in 1936 to make way for the Gaumont Cinema. This postcard was apparently published by Triggs for sending messages to customers, etc.

11. Another example of a shop using a postcard for advertising purposes, is this 1904 picture of Dunn and Son's premises in South Street. At that time girls were taken on as apprentice shop assistants and were expected to live on the premises in rooms on the top floor.

12. I understand that these are Mr. Ferry, the bootmaker, and his sons outside their premises in the Hornet. The advertisement for the Picturedrome would indicate that this was taken in the early 1930's.

13. The Picturedrome Cinema was in South Street and was demolished when the Plaza, later the Odeon, was built in 1935. The cinema's entrance can be seen in this picture, taken in 1929. The horse-drawn band were publicising a garden fete to be held in the grounds of the Bishop's Palace. They are outside Saunders, the irongmongers, a shop that can be seen in the earlier picture of South Street.

14. Pooles, the other cinema in Chichester, was located in the Corn Exchange, now MacDonalds. In this 1913 picture, the façade was dressed overall to celebrate the coronation of George VI.

15. This postcard by Morey, taken at about the same time as the previous one, shows 'Gala Night at Pooles'. I imagine that the lady in the front row with what appears to be her cat on her head was unpopular with those further back.

16. Morey took this picture of a socialist rout, or rally, in Eastgate Square in 1907. There seems to be a considerable police presence. In the background can be seen St. Pancras Church and the Eastgate Hand Laundry in the same building we saw later to be occupied by Mr. Triggs.

17. A series of postcards, depicting Chichester election scenes, were published by Scribb. This one was taken in East Street from the Unionist Party Headquarters, over the International Stores, now Superdrug. Possibly the crowd had gathered to hear a speech from the first-floor windows.

18. Another picture from the same series, showing the crowd dispersing after the declaration of the results, which would have been announced from the Council House in North Street. It is noticeable how few ladies are present, it being of course before the days of female suffrage. Another chance to see Egbert Moore's shopfront.

GENERAL ELECTION, 1924—Chichester Division.

WORK HAS WON, HURRAH!
The RESULT.

COURTAULD (Conservative)	-	20,710
RUDKIN (Liberal)	-	12,416
HOPE (Socialist)	-	1,765

Conservative Majority - 8,294

Printed & Published by T. G. Willis & Co., East St., Chichester

19. I cannot claim that Mr. Green (right) was a relative, but he was certainly an optimist to put himself up as a worker's candidate in Chichester.
The card on the left published after the 1924 General Election, shows that political allegiances have changed little over the years.

20. As befits a road that ran alongside the Barracks, the houses in the Broadway were given names commemorating famous British generals, among them Burgoyne, Kitchener, Roberts, Napier and Gordon.

21. A picture, dated 1908, of the north end of Tower Street with the North Walls in the distance. The gateway on the left led into The Grange, a spectacular Victorian house, built in Gothic style, which was demolished in 1962.

22. This card is undated, but shows a scene that did not change for many years. Despite the title on this card, most Cicestrians knew this as the Westgate Fields. It was an idyllic spot with cattle grazing right up to the city walls, the Cathedral spire forming the backdrop. One cannot help feeling a sense of loss when one looks at the college, the leisure centre and that new car park that are now sited in the fields, soon to be joined by Tesco's supermarket.

23. Other than the presence of the carefully posed children, there has been little change since 1907, when this picture of College Lane was taken. On the card it is called Love Lane, this, however, never being more than a local nickname, the derivation of which is obvious. The thatched cottage is all that remains of the Old Pest House which formed an annexe to the workhouse in Broyle Road.

24. Near to College Lane, in Spitalfields Lane, are a group of council-built houses which I always remember being called the 'tin huts'. I have recently found out the reason why. Apparently, they replaced a dozen or so prefabricated huts, built in 1920 as temporary accommodation to house families on the council's list.

25. This postcard, showing the front of Bishop Otter College, was sent in 1915 by one of the student teachers at the college to her parents in Brighton. She noted that she had been exploring Chichester and district on her bicycle. An insight into parent and daughter relationships of the time is shown in the way in which she signed the card: 'Yours sincerely, Ethel.'

26. What better to send home to impress one's friends than a picture of the science laboratory in the college. One can see some of the facilities provided for the students in 1908. There are gas taps at each of the benches, a fume cupboard in the corner and an open fireplace alongside the lecturer's desk.

27. The outside of the college chapel can be seen in the earlier picture. This internal view shows that there was seating for about a hundred worshippers.

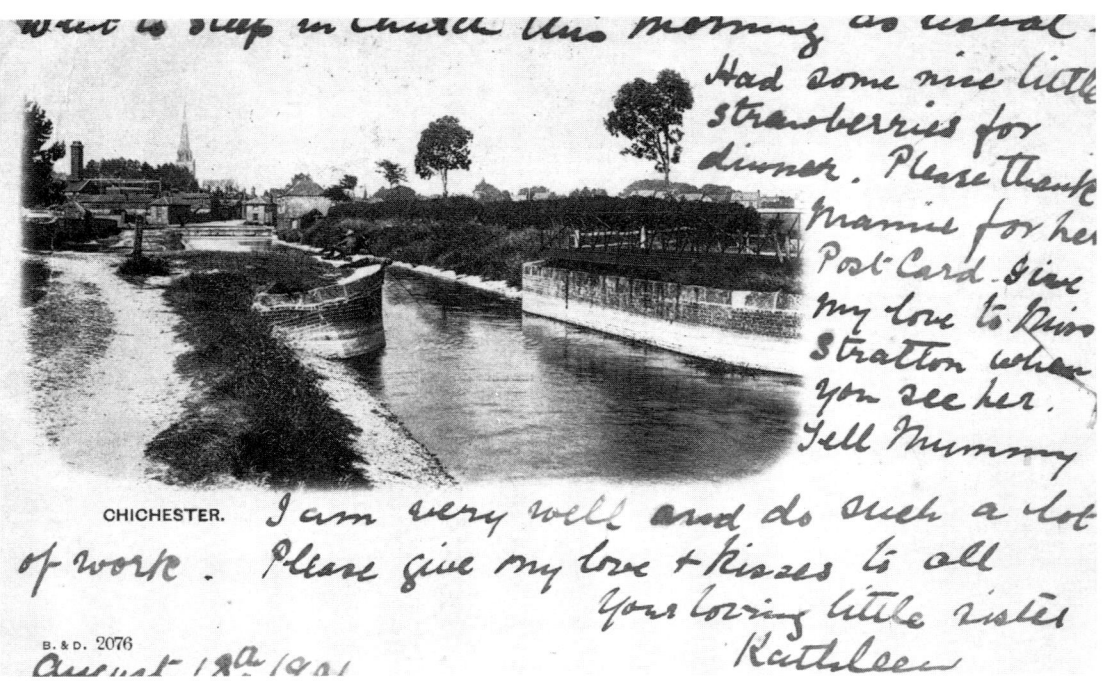

28. Sometimes the message on the card is as interesting as the picture. I fancy that this card, dated 1901, was sent by a student of the college. Showing Chichester Canal, it was sent from Chichester to a Miss Peggy Scott in Maidstone.

29. A final picture from Bishop Otter College of the lecture hall with its gas lighting and the floor marked out for indoor games, possibly badminton. The footnote by the sender tells of other activities enjoyed by the students.

30. An early view of the Chichester market on market day, which has been held since medieval times on a Wednesday. In the distance can be seen the buildings of Eastgate Square.

31. A picture taken in the Market, that seems a strange subject for a postcard, two lorries belonging to Westhampnett Rural District Council, predecessor to Chichester R.D.C. The building in the background, in need of some repair, is the Eastgate Chapel.

32. Behind their bakery and confectionery shop in the Hornet, Messrs. J. Voke & Sons had a tea garden, a popular summer venue for outdoor functions.

33. Voke's shop can be seen in this view of the Eastgate Brewery Inn. Outside the premises, on the right, is Mr. Jim Smith, the landlord. Also shown in the picture are the Bush Inn and the Half Moon Inn, later to become the British Legion Club. The shop next to the arch was Rapson's, the butcher's.

25 CHICHESTER. — West Street and Market Cross. — R. B. — W.

34. The Dolphin and the Anchor were separate establishments until 1910, when Trust House Hotels amalgamated them. The earliest known record of the Dolphin is in 1649 and of the Anchor in 1716. This postcard view is dated 1908. The number of impressive cabs with white-coated drivers outside, may indicate that is was taken in Goodwood week.

35. Another view of the Anchor, taken about the same time. Both the Anchor and the Dolphin had been coaching inns. It is clear that the landlords had been quick to see the new business opportunities of catering for the motorist.

36. A picture of the Globe Hotel in Southgate. This establishment was founded by Thomas Purchase in about 1840 to cater for travellers arriving at the then newly built nearby railway station.

37. A later postcard of the Globe with some of the staff proudly lined up outside. It is apparent that part of the building has been demolished since the earlier postcard.

38. This picture shows another Globe Inn. This one was on the Portsmouth Road at Old Fishbourne, some four miles west of the city and is now a private house.

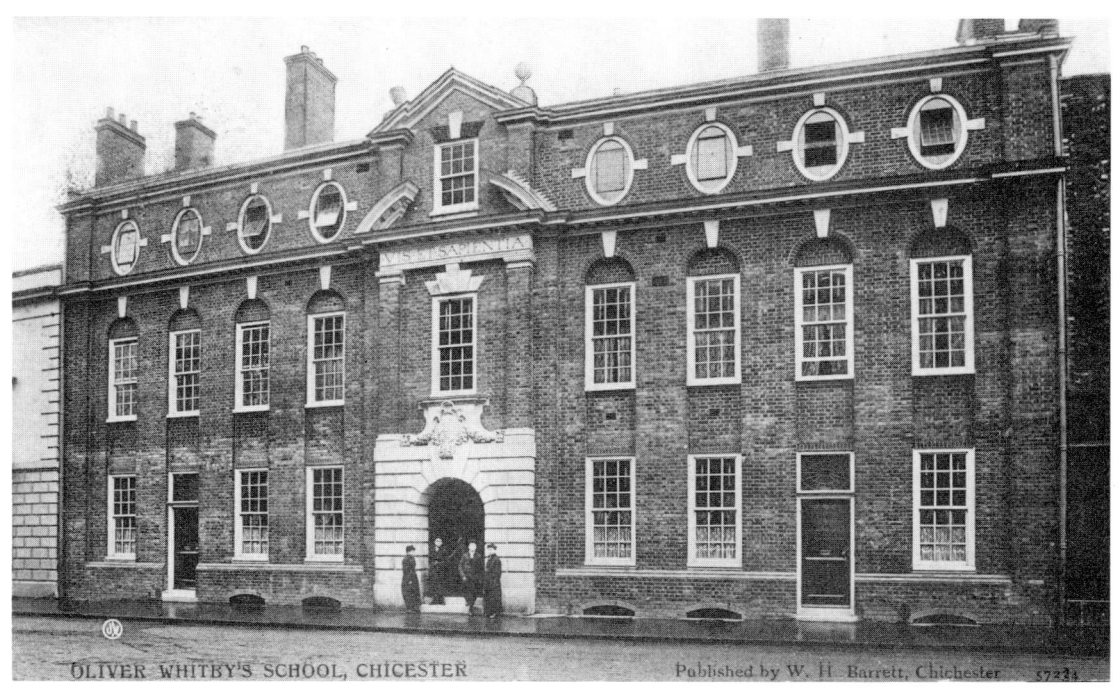

39. This postcard, showing the Oliver Whitby School in West Street, was produced in 1907. The building, which was erected in 1900, has probably not been appreciated by Cicestrians for the outstanding edifice it is. It was designed by Sir Reginald Blomfield, who was also the architect of Graylingwell Hospital. The school was founded in 1702 to provide an education for boys from Chichester and the villages of Harting and Wittering. It closed in 1956 when its funds were used to endow scholarships at Christ's Hospital. The building is now part of the Army Navy store.

40. For many years the Lavant course overflowed, flooding properties in St. Pancras. In this picture the floodwater has extended down New Park Road, covering the graveyards in the foreground. The Sussex Central School was built in 1812.

41. The school building, shown in the previous picture, was demolished in 1880 to make way for the Central Boys' School. When the school moved to premises in Orchard Street in 1974, the building was converted into its present use as a community centre.

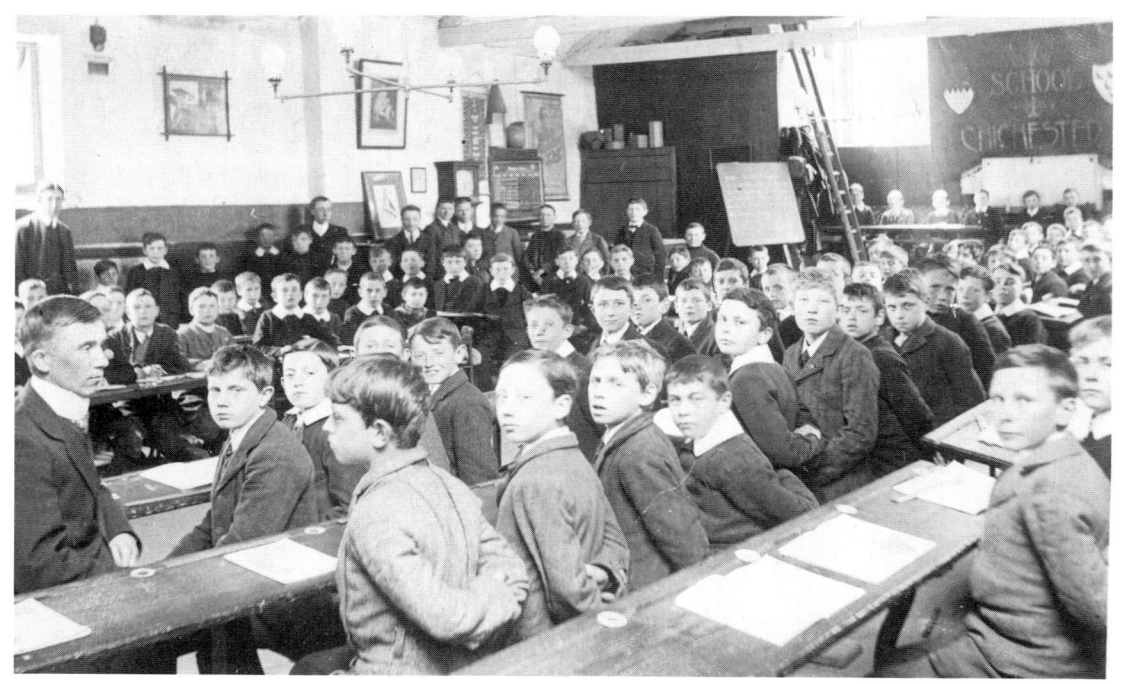

42. On leaving the Central School, many boys went on to the Lancastrian School. In this 1910 picture, one feels that the discipline may have been far more strict than that imposed today.

43. The caption on this picture says: 'Chichester High Schools, Pageant in Priory Park, July 1933, Triumphs of Time, surrender of the Britons to the Romans, Cognidubnus (Mervyn Down) offers a tribute to a Centurian (Bill Weld).'

44. A picture, again by Morey, of the Priory Park pavilion in 1908. The occasion was the annual sports day that took place in the park in which many of the local sports clubs participated. It usually ended with a lantern parade and fireworks display.

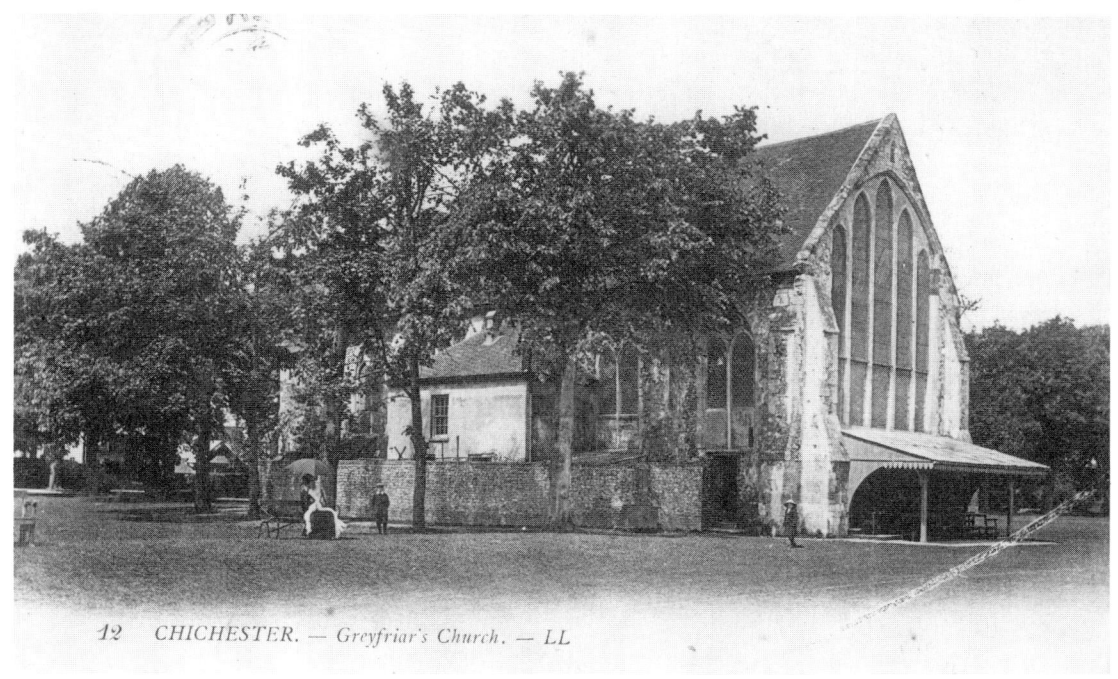

45. The Guildhall in Priory Park was formerly the chapel to the Greyfriars Monastery that stood on the site of the park. Since then, it has been used as a courthouse, a guildhall and now as a museum. In its time, men have been ordained as priests, elected to Parliament and sentenced to death within its walls. This postcard is dated 1916.

46. The winners of the Tug-of-War event at the Priory Park sports in 1913 were this team from Henty's Westgate Brewery. One can imagine that manhandling barrels of ale for a living gave them an unassailable advantage.

47. Knight's football team, 1907. Charles Knight was a printer with premises at No. 12, East Street.

48. Chichester North End Football Club 1910-1911. I have not managed to find out much about this team, except that they played locally from about 1906 to the outbreak of war in 1914.

49. The Chichester Company of the Church Lads Brigade, assembled in their drill hall with members of the band in the front row. Notice that some of the boys are holding rifles, possibly only replicas for drill purposes.

FUNERAL OF MR E E STREET,

50. The funeral of Mr. Eugene Street took place in October 1913. He was a local magistrate, a member of many of Chichester's societies and founding superintendent of the St. John's Ambulance Brigade, it is they who are leading the procession. The building in the centre of the picture was the offices of Arnold, Cooper & Tomkins, solicitors. Mr. Cooper was the coroner for the district and also, having succeeded Mr. Arnold, the city's town clerk.

51. A rare postcard, showing the Chichester Fire Brigade with their horse-drawn fire engine. The Merryweather engine of this type was produced from about 1850 to the end of the nineteenth century.

52. This picture was taken in Bognor Road and shows the Chichester Steam Laundry in the background.

53. This card advertises Mr. Wellcome's 'car for hire'. The business developed into a taxi service, the Wellcome family were also well-known local builders.

54. Both car and carriage can be seen in this fine card from Valentine's taken at the turn of the century. On the left are the shops of E.H. Lewis, watchmaker, and Guy Reynolds, whose sign proclaimed him as 'The City Hatter'.

55. The city attracts many thousands of tourists and holidaymakers every year, most of them paying at least one visit to the Cathedral. It follows therefore, that pictures of the building, its precincts and monuments have always been popular subjects for postcards. This fine view shows the Cathedral seen from the grounds of the Bishop's Palace.

56. Accompanied by his Verger, the Dean walks each day from the deanery to the Cathedral along St. Richard's Walk. The publisher of this card has described the City's patron saint as 'Sir Richard', I have seen others calling him 'King Richard'.

57. A picture of the gate to the Bishop's Palace. The room above is reputed to have been used to detain those, who had offended the ecclesiastical authorities.

58. This doorway on the south side of the Cathedral, which has now been reopened, dates back to the time of the Normans. The chevron, or dog tooth, ornamentation is typical of their style.

59. The bell tower of the Cathedral dates back to the later years of the 14th century. It contains a peal of eight bells, the oldest dating to 1583. Chichester is the only Cathedral in the country with a bell tower separate from the main building.

60. This sculpted reredos, or altar screen, was erected in the Cathedral in 1870 and removed in 1911 to make way for a less ornate wooden screen. This, in turn, has been covered with the Piper Tapestry, that can be seen today.

61. This picture shows the altar in All Saints' Church at Portfield. This church closed in the 1970's, after remaining empty for some years, it was converted for use as a mechanical music museum. The reredos shown in the previous picture was transferred to St. Saviour's Church in Brighton. When this church closed, the reredos was re-erected in the Portfield Museum. Appropriately the church also dates from 1870.

62. The choir of All Saints', Portfield in 1928. Alfred Sivyer, who lent me this picture, is second from left in the second row from the front. He is able to name everyone in the picture.

63. One is sometimes lucky enough to find samples of the portrait cards taken by local photographers. Unfortunately, it is seldom possible to find out more about the subjects. These cards by Thomas Russell date from about 1890.

64. I have been unable to date this picture, taken from under the Cross. One can see horse-drawn traffic in East Street, but the policeman appears to be wearing a fairly modern hat. Note the small cannon under the arch on the left and what I believe is a lamplighter's pole just behind the constable.

65. There are many postcards, showing royal visits to the city, often taking place during the first week in August, it being no coincidence that this was also Goodwood Week. In this picture, one can see the crowds in East Street in 1906, awaiting the carriage of Edward VII. I am not sure if there is any significance in that a shop on the left is displaying the Japanese national flag.

66. Their wait has been rewarded; the King's carriage rounds the Cross where he pauses to receive loyal greetings from the mayor and other dignatories. I am not sure if the lady with the King is Queen Alexandra, or maybe a lady-in-waiting.

67. The crowd have seen their monarch and are departing. The policemen are returning to the police station in Southgate. This picture was taken from the 'West Sussex Gazette' office in South Street. Clearly to be seen, is Bishop's, the bootmaker's shop, decorated for the occasion.

68. A picture which appears to have been taken on the same day by another photographer. I have not been able to discover where from. The royal carriage, with its four horses, has now gained two footmen in the rear, but I cannot see who is in control of the horses.

69. In this picture, King George V is seen in 1913, re-opening the Royal West Sussex Hospital, after extensive alterations and extensions. It was at this visit that the title of 'Royal' was added to the hospital's name. The new out-patients' department can be seen in the background.

70. This picture, taken just before the official opening, shows the front of the hospital with 'Infirmary' on the pediment over the main entrance. In later pictures, it can be seen that the hospital's new title was soon proudly displayed.

71. This postcard was taken at the rear of the hospital during the renovations. Several of the workmen responsible have broken off from their work to pose for the photographer. I wonder if any of them were introduced to the King on the opening day.

72. King Edward VII often stayed at West Dean House during his visits to West Sussex and the Goodwood Races. The owner, Mr. William James, gave £10,000 towards the reconstruction of the Royal West Sussex Hospital as a memorial to King Edward.

73. Goodwood Racecourse, a picture taken from the Trundle in 1935, showing the paddock on the right and the old grandstand before the building of the members' stand, both of which have since been demolished to make way for the present structures.

74. As we have left the City in the last two cards I will take the opportunity to show two delightful pictures taken in the village of Lavant. Chichester was a popular centre for those wishing to visit the outlying villages and there are many cards showing rural scenes. Here the river Lavant flows through the village, with the bridge in the background.

75. Taken from a spot near to that in the previous card, this picture shows the dipping of sheep taking place in the river. Hence the name Sheepwash Lane.

76. To finish, I'd like to show one of the many greetings postcards that picture views of the City. This one was sent to a friend as a Christmas card in 1909, by a lady signing herself 'affectionately Rose'.